The purpose of this book is to provide a step-by-step approach to practicing and mastering **Beethoven's Für Elise.**

Many pianists today do not know how to practice the piano efficiently and hours of valuable practice time are wasted. This book will help you learn the music thoroughly, protect you from unnecessary wasteful practicing, and make the best use of your practice time.

Please note that this book is only meant to serve as a guide. There are many different ways to practice and every pianist has their own ideal practice routine. Feel free to skip exercises that you feel may be unnecessary for your skill level and feel free to add variations and exercises that you feel will personally benefit you. However, do not get into a habit of practicing a passage the same way over and over again. The fastest progress is made when a passage is practiced in many different ways from many different angles exercising both the fingers and the mind.

Part 1: "A" Section
(mm. 1 to 23)

1. Learn the Right Hand (mm. 1 - 2):

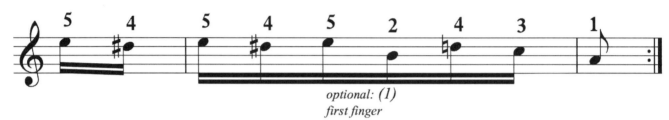

2. Practice it in different ways:

3. Add legato:

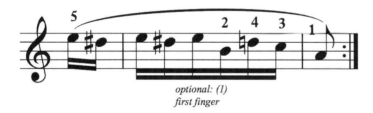

✓ *Keep your fingers curved*
✓ *Keep your wrist low*
✓ *Do not let your finger joints collapse*

4. Add a crescendo to the first five notes...............and a diminuendo to the last four notes:

5. Practice introducing the Left Hand:

6. Learn the Left Hand (mm. 2 - 4):

7. Practice it different ways:

8. Learn the Right Hand (mm. 2 - 4):

9. Practice it different ways:

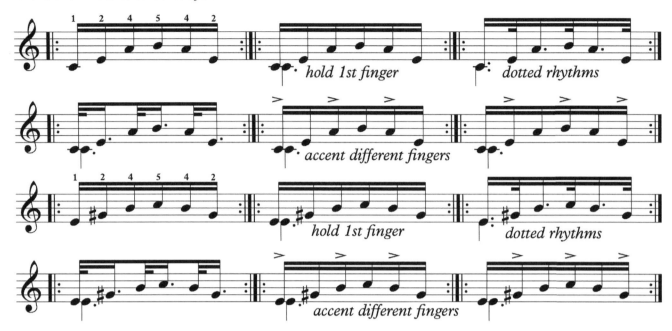

10. Focus on each arpeggio separately:

11. Practice transitions from one harmony to another:

12. Put (mm. 2 - 4) together:

Examine the Harmonic Progression for (mm.1 - 8):

Practice using the pedal:

Hold down the pedal until you play the first note of a new harmony

Release, and then put the pedal down quickly to hold the new harmony

13. Practice pedaling (mm. 1 - 8):

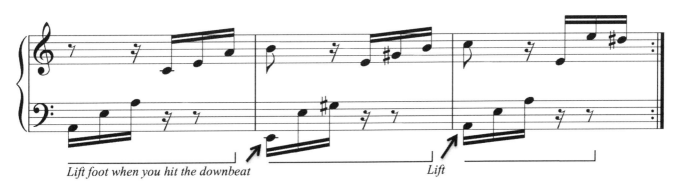

6

14. Start from the beginning and add pedal:

Don't move ahead until mm. 1 - 8 have been mastered!
Go back and repeat No. 1 - 14 if needed

15. Learn the Left Hand (mm. 10 - 13):

16. Practice it different ways:

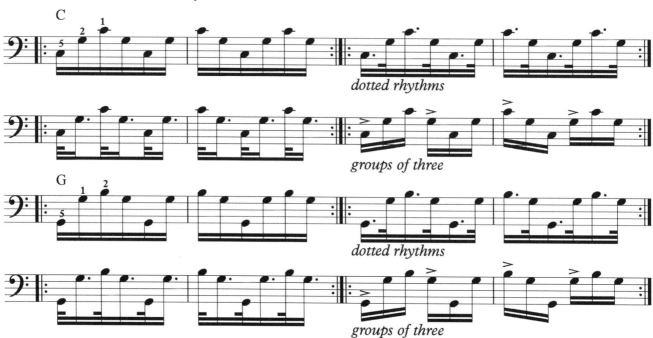

✓ *Practice accuracy over speed*
✓ *Always relax your hands, arms, and shoulders*

Really focus on:

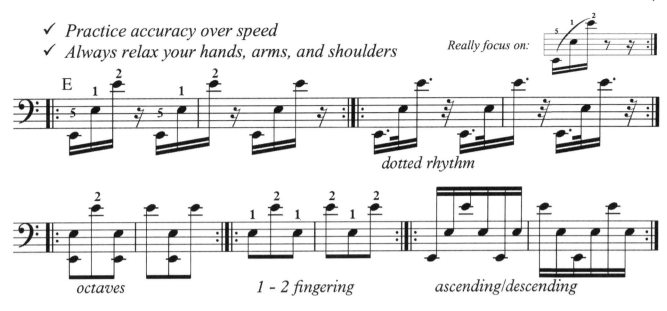

dotted rhythm

octaves   *1 - 2 fingering*   *ascending/descending*

17. Learn the Right Hand (mm. 9 - 13):

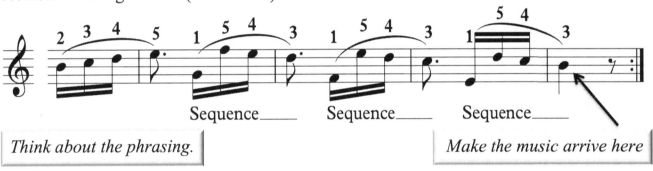

Sequence_____   Sequence_____   Sequence_____

Think about the phrasing.   *Make the music arrive here*

18. Practice it in different ways:

dotted rhythm

with sixths

accent different fingers

19. Add the LH Root:

Fifth finger on every root:

20. Put both hands together:

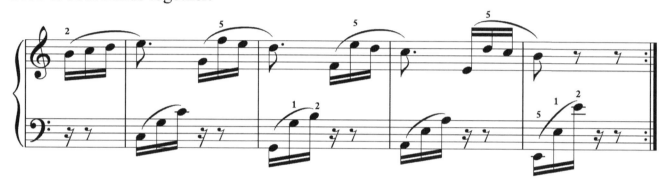

21. Practice the Octaves (mm. 13 - 14):

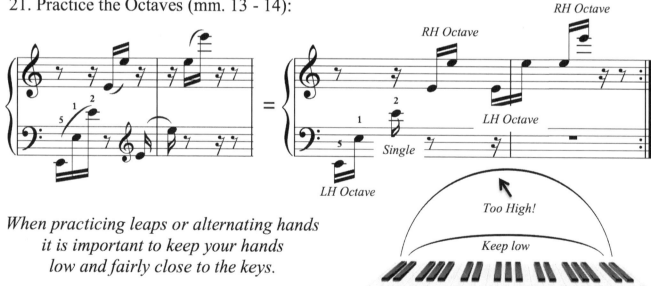

*When practicing leaps or alternating hands
it is important to keep your hands
low and fairly close to the keys.*

22. Practice Alternating Hands (mm. 14 - 16):

23. Practice (mm. 13 - 14) in different ways:

octaves *broken octaves*

dotted rhtyhm

24. Practice (mm. 14 - 16) in different ways: *(Down-stems = Left Hand, Up-stems = Right Hand)*

dotted rhythms

accent different fingers

25. Practice (mm. 13 - 16):

10

Examine the Harmonic Progression for (mm. 9 - 16):

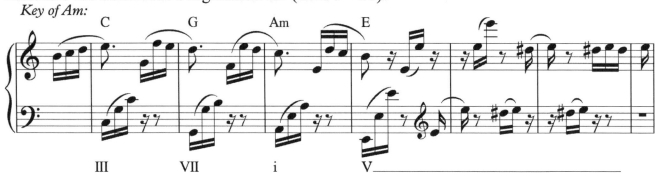

26. Put the sections together (mm. 9 - 16):

Don't move ahead until mm. 9 - 16 have been mastered!
Go back and repeat No. 14 - 26 if needed

Examine the Form for (mm. 1 - 23); Ternary ABA

27. Put it all together (mm 1- 23):

- ✓ Focus on Dynamics
- ✓ Focus on Legato playing
- ✓ Focus on Fingerings
- ✓ Focus on Pedaling
- ✓ Focus on Repeat signs

12

28. Play with Metronome: ♩ = 70 .... Gradually increase to ♩ = 150

Metronome Beat = ⬇

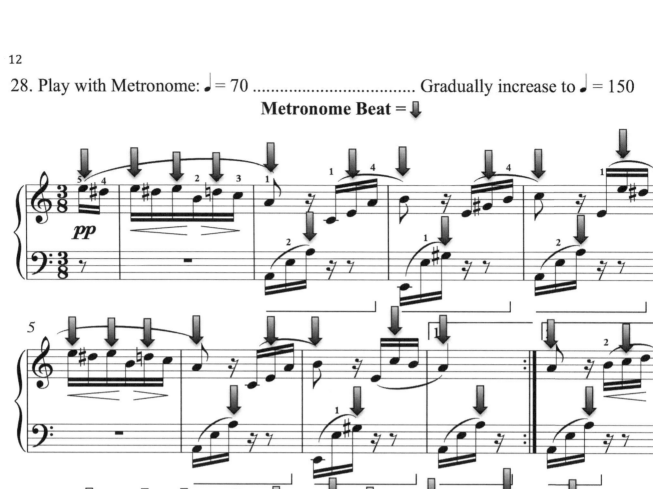

29. Play with Metronome: ♩· = 40 .... Gradually increase to ♩· = 50

Metronome Beat = ⬇

14

Study the musical phrases: Where is the music going?

Think about the big picture!

15

30. Work on Musical Phrasing: (*The given phrasing is only a suggestion*)

Be Expressive! Give the music purpose and direction!

31. Check List for (mm. 1-23):

- ✓ **Technique:** note accuracy, finger dexterity, use of pedal, slips?, hesitations?
- ✓ **Tone Quality:** smooth legato, clarity of touch, balance, false accents?
- ✓ **Interpretation:** confidence, fluency, shape and direction,
- ✓ **Other Factors:** stage presence, appearance, artistry, musically satisfying?

Part 2: "B" Section
(mm. 24 to 39)

1. Learn the Right Hand (mm. 24 - 25):

2. Practice it different ways:

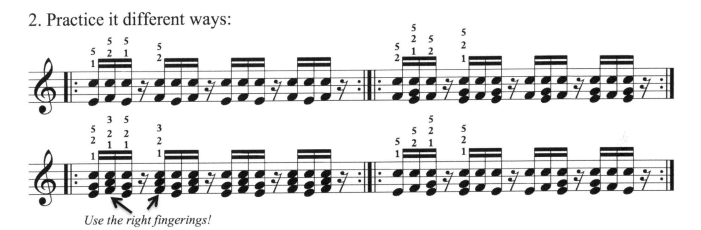

Use the right fingerings!

3. Focus on bringing out the lower voice:

Here are different ways to practice it:

✓ *Make sure fingers are curved and strong!*

When trying to voice certain notes it is important not to push! Drop the weight of your hand on the desired fingers.

4. Learn the Left Hand (mm. 24 - 25):

5. Practice it different ways:

6. Focus on bringing out the bass line:

Bring out

Here are different ways to practice it:

✓ *Curved fingers*

Drop the weight of your hand on every finger that carries the bass line.

Examine the Harmony for (mm. 24 - 25):

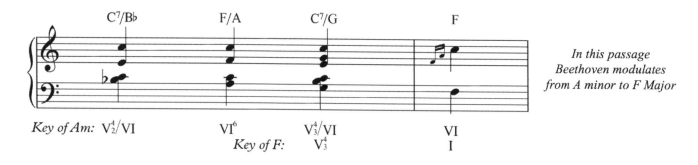

In this passage Beethoven modulates from A minor to F Major

7. Alternate between right hand and left hand:

8. Slowly start practicing both hands: ♩ = 80 .... Gradually increase to ♩ = 160

Bring out top voice

Bring out the bass line

> It is important to be be mentally calm and physically relaxed when practicing.

9. Practice both hands in different ways: Clarity over speed!

Use the right fingering on the F chord (3-2-1)

10. Phrase the transition:

Make it sound like you arrived someplace new

20

11. Learn the Left Hand (mm. 25 - 33):

Examine the Harmonic Progression for (mm. 25 - 33):

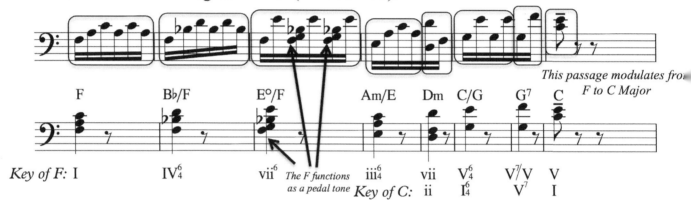

This passage modulates from F to C Major

Key of F: I   IV$_4^6$ vii^6 *The F functions as a pedal tone*   iii$_4^6$ vii   V$_4^6$ V^7/V   V

Key of C: ii   I$_4^6$ V^7 I

12. Practice (mm. 25 - 26) in different ways:

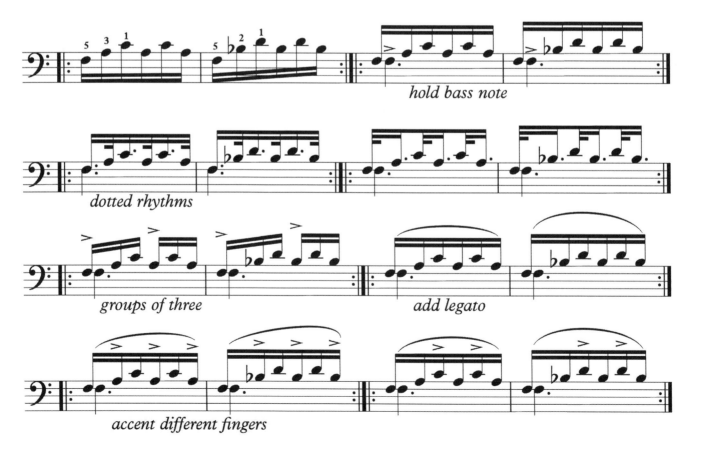

hold bass note

dotted rhythms

groups of three   *add legato*

accent different fingers

13. Practice (mm. 27) in different ways:

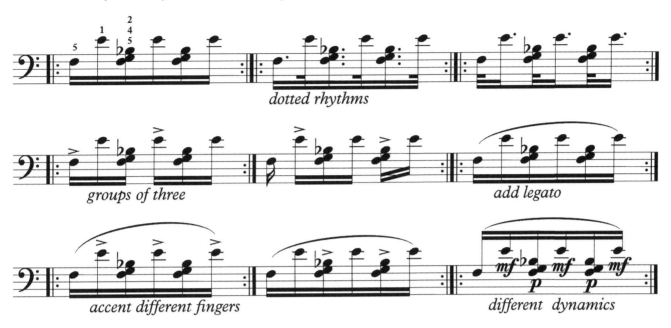

dotted rhythms

groups of three

add legato

accent different fingers

different dynamics

14. Practice finger pedaling:

Holding down the bass note gives illusion of using pedal

Hold   Hold   Hold where you can   Hold   Hold

15. Practice (mm. 28 - 30) in different ways:

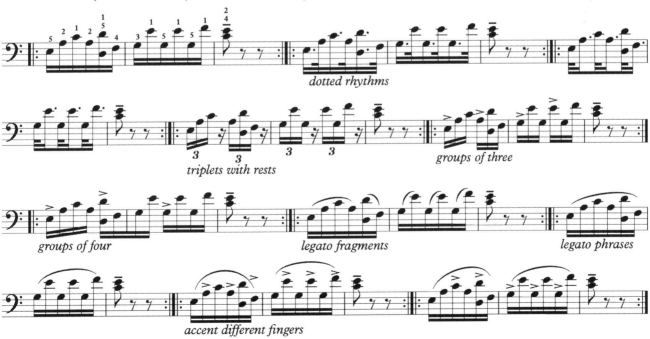

dotted rhythms

triplets with rests   groups of three

groups of four   legato fragments   legato phrases

accent different fingers

16. Put (mm. 25 - 33) together: Make two distinct phrases

Phrase 1   *Phrase 2*

17. Learn the Right Hand (mm. 25 - 33):

18. Practice the 4-3 finger change:

out of time   *dotted rhythms*

together

19. Practice the descending scale:

dotted rhythms

groups of three

groups of 2 + 3   *groups of 3 + 2*

20. Practice appoggiatura, thirty-second notes, and finger change:

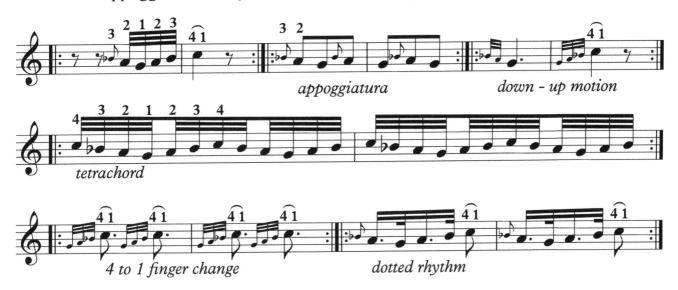

appoggiatura

down - up motion

tetrachord

4 to 1 finger change

dotted rhythm

21. Practice the suspension and release:

second note is softer

softer

22. Hands together with Right Hand downbeats:

23. Hands together with Left Hand downbeats:

24. Practice playing the notes that fall on the 3/8 time:

Don't ignore fingerings!

25. Practice (mm. 24 - 32): Don't use pedal!

Don't move ahead until mm. 24 - 36 have been mastered!
Go back and repeat No. 1 - 25 if needed

26. Learn the Left Hand (mm. 32 - 33):

Remember to relax as you practice. Eliminate all tension in hands, arms, and shoulders.

27. Practice it in different ways:

Notice that (mm. 24 - 25) and (mm. 32 - 33) have a similar pattern.

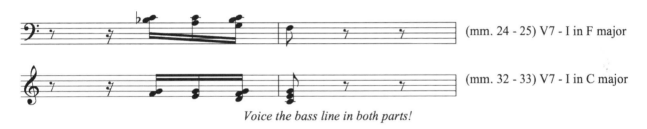

(mm. 24 - 25) V7 - I in F major

(mm. 32 - 33) V7 - I in C major

Voice the bass line in both parts!

28. Learn the Left Hand (mm. 32 - 36):

staccato!   *staccato!*

29. Practice the leap in (mm. 33 and 35):

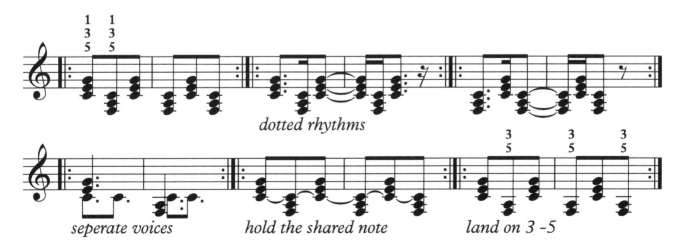

dotted rhythms

seperate voices   *hold the shared note*   *land on 3 -5*

30. Learn the Right Hand (mm. 32 - 36):

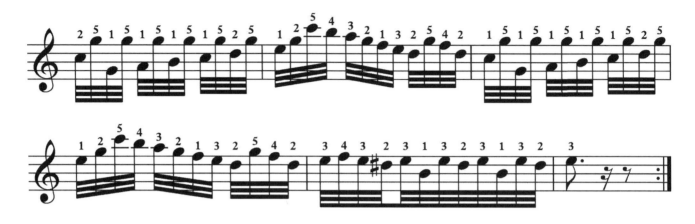

31. Practice it in different ways:

(mm. 34 - 36)

dotted rhythms

groups of three

32. Focus on the Melody (mm. 32 - 36):

Your thumb needs to create the melodic phrase

33. Bring out the melody:

Strong 1st finger and light 5th finger

Bring out

Bring out

34. Hands together without the off beats (mm. 32 - 33):

Make the music arrive here

35. With off beats:

36. Practice without (mm. 33 and 35) in the Right Hand:

   ✓ *Relax your shoulders, arms, hands, wrists*
   ✓ *Play slowly before playing quickly*
   ✓ *Avoid repeating mistakes as much as you can*
   ✓ *Be nice to yourself even if you make a mistake*

37. Practice without (mm. 32 and 34) in the Right Hand:

38. Practice with metronome: ♪ = 70 .... Gradually increase to ♪ = 150

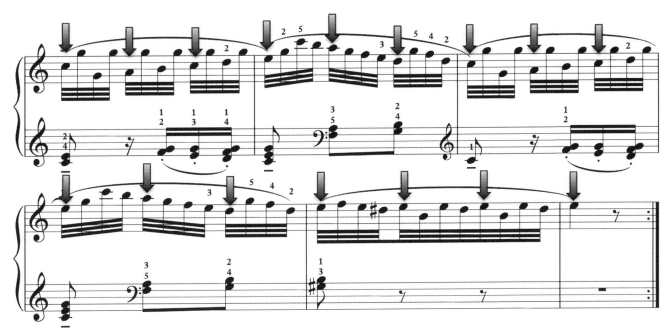

Study the Harmonic Progression for (mm. 32 - 37):

The E chord modulates the passage back to the key of A minor

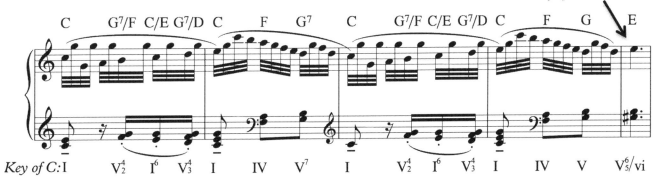

39. Practice (mm. 32 - 41): Don't forget the dynamics!

Don't move ahead until mm. 32 - 36 have been mastered!
Go back and repeat No. 26 - 39 if needed

Examine the Form for (mm. 24 - 37); Binary AB

(mm 24 - 31) A:

(mm. 32 - 37) B:

Look at the big picture for (mm. 1 - 61); Ternary ABA

mm. 1-23 Ternary ABA

mm. 24-37 Binary AB

mm. 38-61 Ternary ABA

40. Put (mm. 24 - 37) together:

41. Focus on transitions (mm. 21 - 25) and (mm. 30 - 33):

*Each transition modulates
into a new key*

42. Put (mm. 24 - 61) together:

43. Play with Metronome: ♩. = 40 .... Gradually increase to ♩. = 50

44. Start from the beginning:

Don't forget about phrasing and musicality!
Be Expressive! Give the music purpose and direction!

- ✓ **Technique:** note accuracy, finger dexterity, use of pedal, slips?, hesitations?, lightness in the wrist, LH staccato vs. RH legato?
- ✓ **Tone Quality:** smooth legato, even staccato, balance between hands, false accents?
- ✓ **Interpretation:** confidence, fluency, shape, direction, convincing transitions?
- ✓ **Other Factors:** stage presence, appearance, artistry, musically satisfying?

Part 3: "C" Section
(mm. 61 to 83)

1. Learn the Left Hand (mm. 61): There are two ways you can play it.

2. Practice it in different ways:

3. Do the same with Bb (mm. 73):

37

4. Do the same with an ascending scale:

dotted rhythms

groups of two

groups of three

Optional Extra Challenge:

groups of four

groups of 2 + 3

groups of 3 + 2

groups of 3 + 4

groups of 4 + 3

groups of 2 + 3 + 4

5. Learn the Left Hand (mm. 66 - 69):

There are two ways to play the repeated double notes;
Arm movement *and* **Wrist movement**

Wrist movement

Arm movement

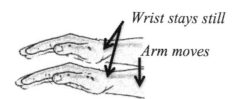

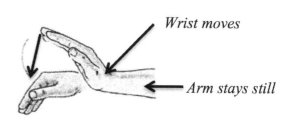

6. Practice it in different ways: Alternate between arm and wrist movement.

dotted rhythms

groups of two

groups of three

groups of 2 + 3

groups of 3 + 2

7. Learn the Right Hand (mm. 62 - 69):

8. Practice bringing out the top voice:

9. Practice in rhythm: Loud on top and quiet on bottom.

10. Learn the Right Hand (mm. 74 - 78):

11. Practice bringing out the top voice:

12. Hands together slowly transitioning from one chord to another (mm 62 - 78):

13. Play the downbeats only (mm. 62 - 78):

42

14. Play the passage in fragments:

Study the Harmonic Progression for (mm. 62 - 78):

A is a pedal tone

Key of Am: vii°⁶/₅/IV   IV⁶   V⁹   i   IV   vii°/V

i⁶/₁₄   V⁷   i   vii°⁶/₅/IV   IV⁶   IV⁶/₄

Key of Am: ♭II   V⁶/₄/♭II   ♭II   vii°⁶/₅/i   i   V
Key of B♭: I   V⁶/₄   I

15. Play with Metronome: ♪ = 70 .... Gradually increase to ♪ = 150

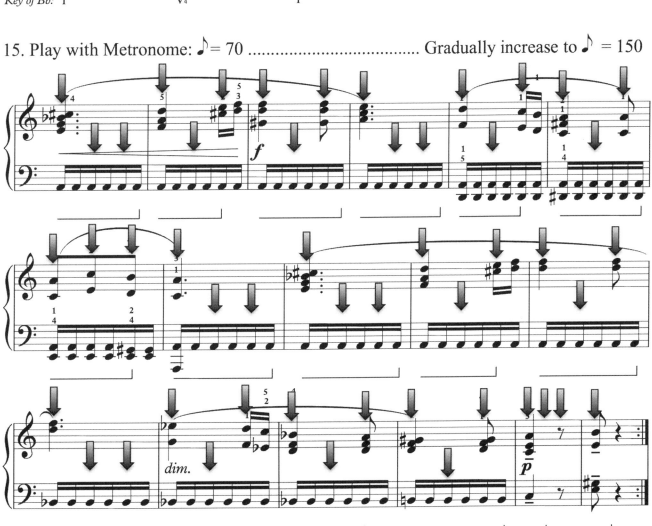

44

16. Play with Metronome at ♩. = 40 .... Gradually increase to ♩. = 50

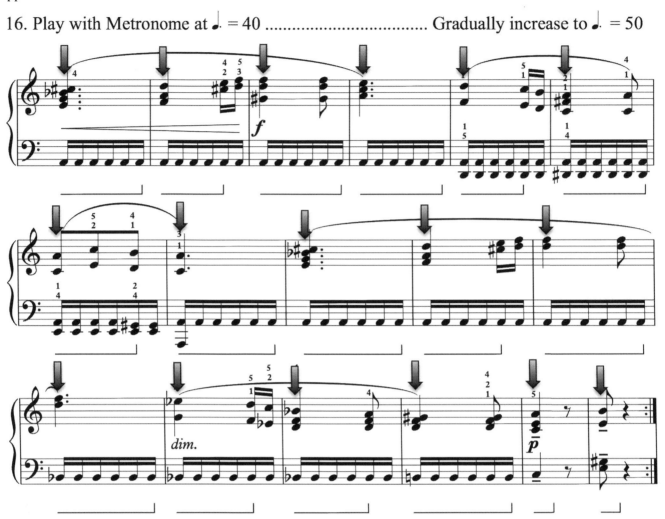

Don't move ahead until mm. 62 - 78 have been mastered!
Go back and repeat No. 1 - 16 if needed

17. Learn the Right Hand (mm. 79 - 84):

18. Practice (mm. 79 - 82) in different ways:

dotted rhythms

groups of two

groups of three

groups of four

19. Practice the crescendo:

As you practice the crescendo think about the musical phrasing.
It will make the crescendo more natural.

20. Learn the Left Hand (mm. 79 - 82)

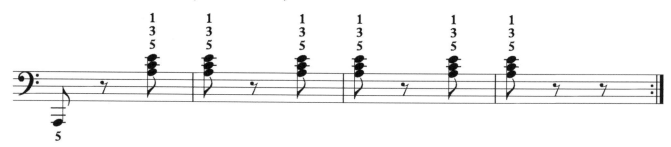

21. Practice the leap:

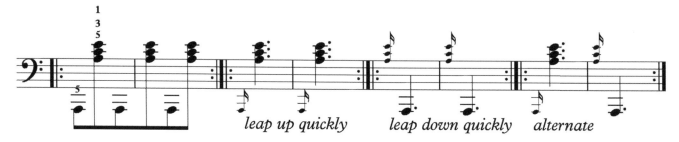

22. Practice Hands together (mm 78 - 82):

23. Isolate and practice the arpeggios:

23. Practice the crescendo with Both Hands:

Do not forget to shape a crescendo in the left hand!

24. Practice (mm. 82 - 84) in different ways:

dotted rhythms

groups of 2

groups of 3

groups of 4

48

25. Practice the diminuendo:

Don't be afraid of starting very loudly!

26. Practice (mm. 82 - 85) with metronome: ♪ = 70 ....Gradually increase to ♪ = 150

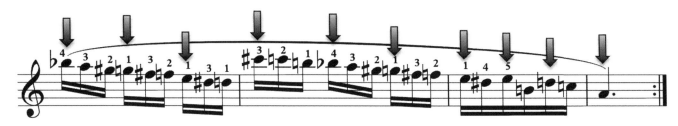

Watch out for the transition from triplet eights to regular eights

27. Practice (mm. 79 - 85) with metronome: ♪ = 70 ....Gradually increase to ♪ = 150

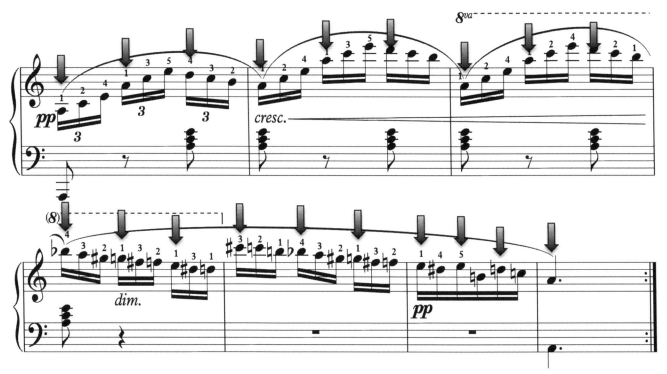

When practicing with metronome continue to focus on phrasing so that the music doesn't become mechanical!

28. Practice with metronome at ♩. = 40 ....Gradually increase to ♩. = 50

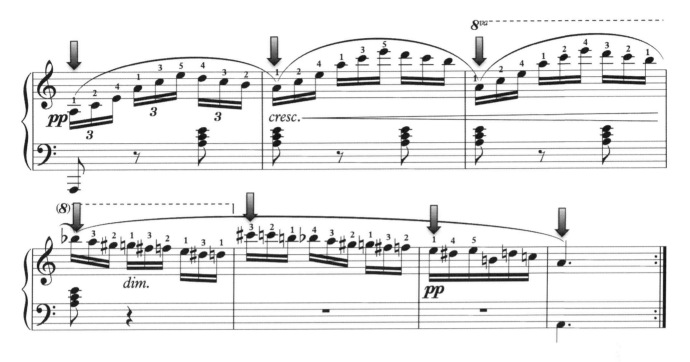

29. Work on the phrasing: *(Move the music forward)*

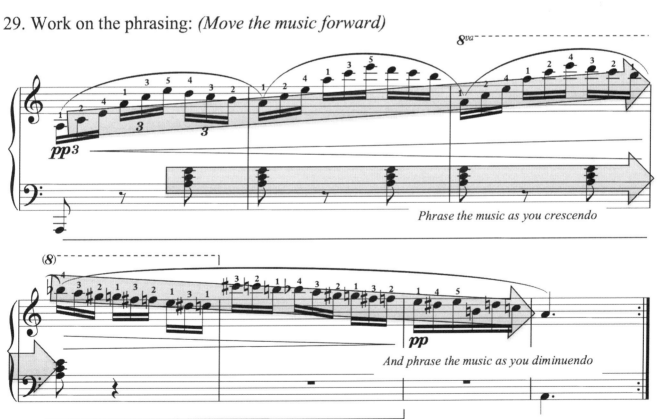

Phrase the music as you crescendo

And phrase the music as you diminuendo

Don't move ahead until mm. 78 - 85 have been mastered!

50

Go back and repeat No. 17 - 28 if needed

Examine the Form for (mm. 61 - 83); Binary AB

(mm 61 - 78) A:

(mm. 79 - 83) B:
(transitional material)

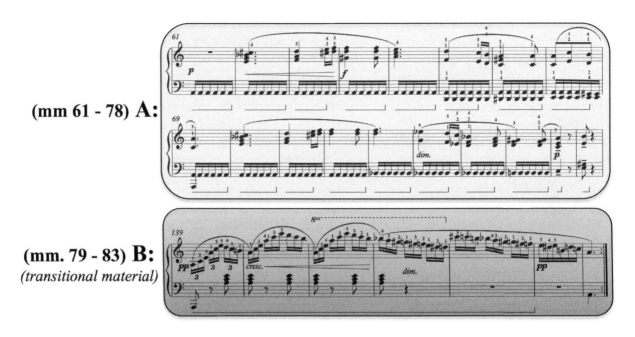

Look at the big picture for (mm. 1 - 105); Rondo ABACA

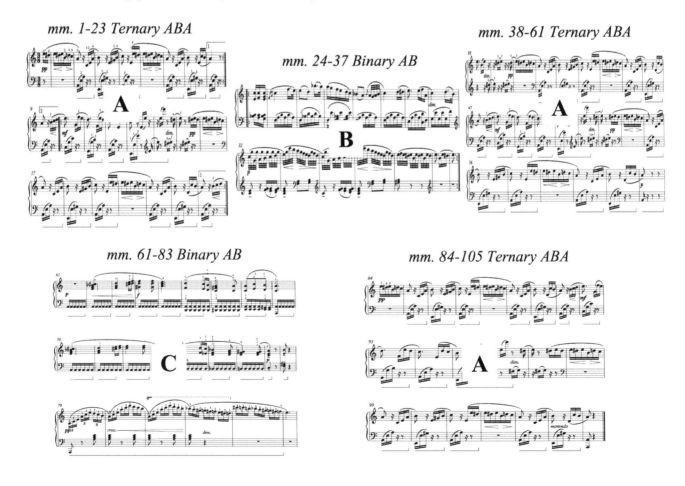

mm. 1-23 Ternary ABA

mm. 24-37 Binary AB

mm. 38-61 Ternary ABA

mm. 61-83 Binary AB

mm. 84-105 Ternary ABA

29. Put (mm. 61 - 85) together:

30. Put (mm. 61 - 105) together:

- ✓ **Technique:** note accuracy, finger dexterity, use of pedal, slips?, hesitations?, lightness in the wrist, arpeggios, chromatic scale.
- ✓ **Tone Quality:** smooth legato, even staccato, even repeated notes, good voicing, steady crescendos, proper diminuendos, balance between hands, false accents?
- ✓ **Interpretation:** confidence, fluency, shape, direction, convincing transition from C section back to A?
- ✓ **Other Factors:** stage presence, appearance, artistry, musically satisfying?

Final Review

Practice section by section: If any weak spots are found go back and review.

(mm. 1 - 8): Part 1, No. 1 - 14

(mm. 9 - 16): Part 1, No. 15 - 26

(mm. 24 - 32): Part 2, No. 1 - 25

(mm. 32 - 41) Part 2, No. 26 - 39

(mm. 61 - 78) Part 3, No. 1 - 16

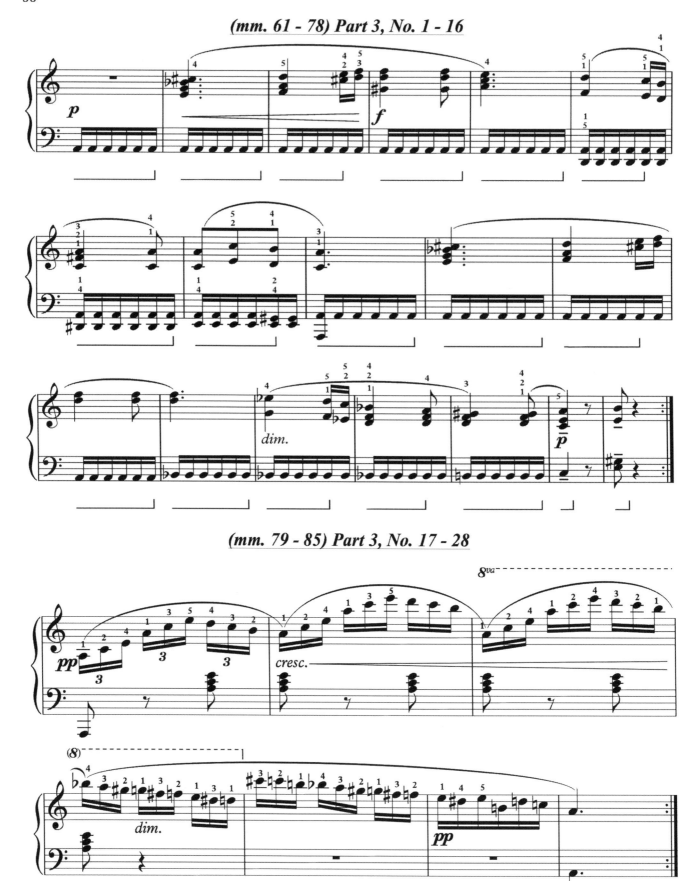

(mm. 79 - 85) Part 3, No. 17 - 28

Practice the entire piece with metronome: ♩. = 40 - 50

60

Focus on large phrases: Work on bringing out the music!

64

Congratulations on getting through the piece!

But Don't Stop!
Continue improving your playing by
bringing out more and more details in the music.
Always try to make the music as beautiful as you can.

The following pages have two versions of Für Elise;
A four page version with a single page turn,
and a two page version with no page turns.

You may use whichever one you are more comfortable with. Enjoy.

Für Elise

Beethoven

Für Elise

Beethoven

Supplementary Exercises

1. (mm. 2 - 4) i-V-i progression in all keys:

2. (mm. 9 - 14) III-VII-i-V progression in all keys:

74

3. (mm. 24 - 25) in ascending sequence: *(starting from C)*

4. (mm. 24 - 25) $V_2^4/VI - VI^6 - V_3^4/VI - VI$
or ($V_2^4 - I^6 - V_3^4 - I$) progression in all keys:

5. (mm. 32 - 41) in ascending sequence:

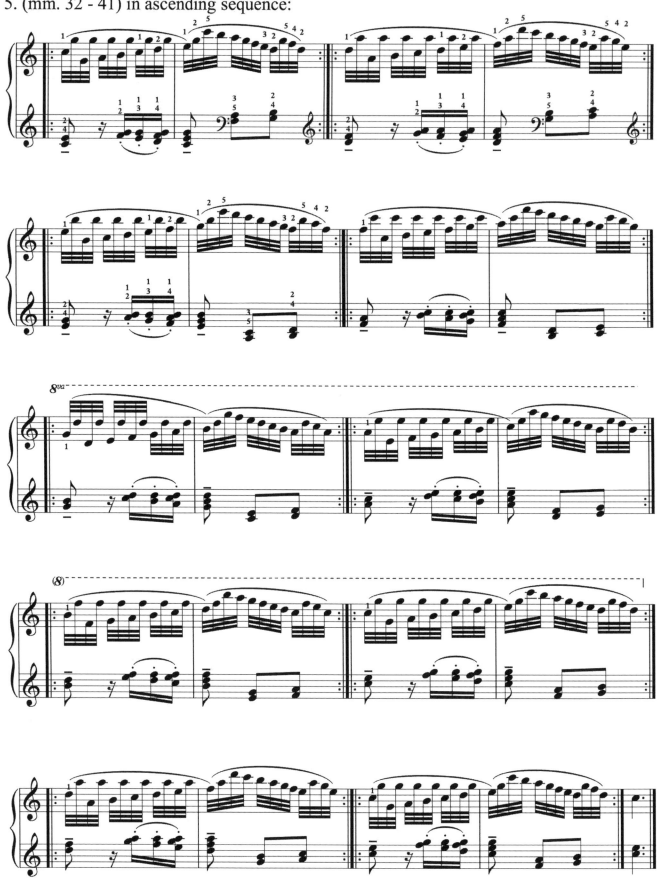

6. (mm. 79 - 82) in ascending sequence: (*starts 1 octave lower*)

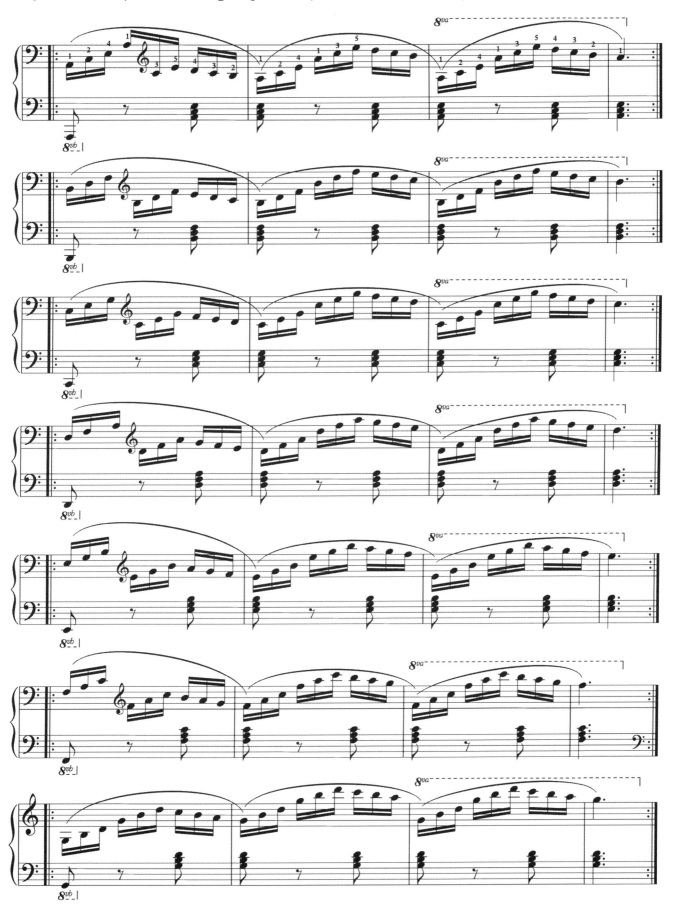

Made in the USA
Middletown, DE
16 October 2021